Xscape AnXiety

How To Overcome Anxiety/Panic Attacks and General Anxiety Disorders

Jonathan R. Powell

Published by Areté Publishing

© Jonathan Powell, 2021

The rights of Jonathan Powell to be identified as the author of this work have been asserted by him in accordance with the Copyright, Designs and Patents Act of 1988.
All rights reserved; no part of this publication may be reproduced, stored in a retrieval system, or transmitted in any form or by any means, electronic, mechanical, photocopying, recording or otherwise without the prior written consent of the publisher or a licence permitting copying in the UK issued by the Copyright Licensing Agency Ltd. www.cla.co.uk

ISBN 978-1-78222-894-3

Photographs: Jonathan Powell

Creative assistant: Victoria Cordell

Book design, layout and production management by Into Print

www.intoprint.net
+44 (0)1604 832149

Xscape Anxiety

Understanding Panic attacks and Anxiety Disorders

The People Who Help People to Help Themselves!

Written by Mr Jonathan R. Powell
Creative assistant Mrs Victoria Cordell

Disclaimer

Reasonable care has been taken to ensure that the information presented in this book is accurate. However, the reader should understand that the information provided within does not constitute legal, medical, or professional advice of <u>any</u> kind.

No Liability: this product is supplied "as is" and without warranties. ALL warranties, express or implied, are hereby disclaimed.

Use of this product constitutes acceptance of the "No Liability" policy. If you do not agree with this policy, you are not permitted to use or distribute this product.

Areté Publishing, employees, associates, distributors, agents, and affiliates shall not be liable for any losses or damages whatsoever (including, without limitation, consequential loss, or damage) directly or indirectly arising from the use of this product.

Whilst the author has taken all reasonable steps to represent an honest and accurate assessment of the subject matter, the views expressed are purely the personal observations of the author and are not meant to be held in law as legally, medically, or scientifically accurate.

Preface

I dedicate this book to all those affected by the current global pandemic and my children who I believe may have inherited their occasional heightened states of anxiety from me. Whilst I would not have chosen that particular trait for them, it is my belief, that a greater understanding of the symptoms and causes will help them become stronger in their outlook and provide them with the confidence of self-determination.

Whether it is a fear of flying or being alone in unknown places, taking exams, work interviews or just prone to over analysing difficult situations (with disastrous results). My hope is that to explore this subject will give anyone who suffers from either Panic Attacks, High levels of Stress or Anxiety will be helped by the knowledge that I have gained either through personal experience or by those whose qualifications on the subject far outweigh my own and to whose contribution I am extremely grateful.

Contents

Dealing with Anxiety Today
    Live in The Moment 9
    Control What You Can Control. 10
    It's Okay to Not Feel Okay 11
    Get Help If You Need It 11

Start at the Beginning!
    Know the Facts 13
    What Are the Physical Signs? 15
    What Are the Symptoms? 18
    Anxiety and Depression 23
    What Causes Panic Attacks? 27
    How to Confront a Panic Attack 28
    Modern Day Stress Triggers. 33
    Alleviating Fears of Anxiety/Panic Attacks 36

Understanding Fear
    Phobias 42
    How to Deal With Phobias .45
    When It's Agoraphobia 45
    Obsessive Compulsive Disorder (OCD) 47
    Cognitive Behaviour Therapy (CBT) 51

Mental Health and Wellbeing
    Anger Management 55
    Anger Management Therapy 62
    Breathe In – Breathe Out 65
    Will I Need Medication? 69

Taking Control and Moving Forward

    Foods That May Enhance Your Anxiety.. 74
    Stress Busting Foods for A Healthier Lifestyle .. .. .80
    Food for Thought.. 83
    Smile With Confidence!.. 91
    Music and Relaxation 93
    Leave Your Job At Work 96
    Exercise and Take Care Of Yourself . .. .97
    Smoking 102

Conclusion .. .. .105

Acknowledgments .. .. .106

Dealing with Anxiety Today

Apart from the normal day to day hustle and stresses of daily living in our modern world, we now have a global pandemic and national/local restrictions to deal with.

Unfortunately, dealing with anxiety has become a part of 'normal' life for many individuals now, and although this problem is not necessarily a new phenomenon, there are certain aspects of modern times that have served to exacerbate the issue.

Due to our world being so connected through our televisions, radio, internet, and social media; people today are not only exposed to the issues in their immediate local environment, but also to all the bad and terrible things taking place across the entire globe. Unfortunately, bad news always makes the headlines.

All this at a time when we are expected to juggle so many more responsibilities, whilst trying to remain sane, productive, and keeping as positive as possible.

Although anxiety certainly varies in intensity and frequency from person to person, there are a few ways to deal with the issue, that are beneficial for anyone experiencing this issue.

The following information covers a few strategies and techniques to alleviate some of your anxiety and hopefully help to improve your overall quality of life.

Live in The Moment

As obvious at it appears to us, the only point in time in which we EVER exist is *right now!* Ironically, most of us tend to dedicate the bulk of our mental energy into the past or future. Anxiety is great at causing us to replay past mistakes in our head and constantly worry about things that have yet to occur. A big part of dealing with anxiety is to live in the moment. This means focusing all our physical and mental energy on what is going on right now. Not only does this simplify life, but it also allows us to get the most out of our limited and precious time. Trying to deal with our entire past and future on a constant basis makes it virtually impossible to appreciate what is right in front of us.

Control What You Can Control

The fact is that many of the issues causing anxieties in our lives, are beyond our control. This includes global and local community issues in addition to problems we may be experiencing in our personal lives.

What we all need to realise is that the weight of the world is **NOT** on any one's individual shoulders, even though it certainly appears that way at times. Anxiety leads our thought processes to consider all these perceived problems and set about solving them – even though they are way out of our hands!

Focusing upon the issues that immediately confront us is where we do have the ability to successfully resolve them. Community and family (Although somewhat limited by restrictions) can also play an important role in this. Working together is so much healthier for all of us, both mentally and physically. Remember, No one individual can solve all the problems of the world.

The adage: -

"A problem shared is a problem halved"

is not only true but has been scientifically shown to reduce stress and improve mental health.

It's Okay to Not Feel Okay

Another side effect of anxiety is the feeling of isolation. People who routinely experience anxiety tend to feel like they are the only ones dealing with this issue.

Because of this perspective, we often feel like everyone else is much happier than we are, and that we won't be accepted if anyone else knew the extent of our anxiety. It is so important to realize that this is far from the truth.

Everyone around us is experiencing some degree of anxiety or mental hang up. You are far from alone. Never feel like it's o.k. to go through life acting as if everything is okay when it isn't.

Get Help If You Need It

If anxiety is something you are having trouble dealing with on your own, then please just don't! There is absolutely nothing wrong with seeking professional help for this issue.

Ironically, until recently our society readily accepted getting help for even a minor physical ailment but sadly not mental health issues. Thankfully there has been a massive sea change in public awareness and acceptance.

Consider this, if you had the flu, you would most certainly seek out a doctor to take care of it. Why would you not see a doctor that is medically trained in alleviating mental health issues? If you are dealing with anxiety there is help available, please get it if you need it!

Finally, with all the current restrictions in place, I know that it can sometimes be difficult to be aware of those in your immediate vicinity that may be living alone or in vulnerable circumstances. I would urge you to try to look out for your neighbours. When was the last time you saw them? Has the milk been taken in, is a there a lot of post still on the doormat? Are they able to drive? If not, could you or someone you know offer to pick something up for them next time you visit the shops or chemist?

You don't have to love your neighbour but offering a helping hand when it's needed (particularly in the present crisis) will I am sure be much appreciated.

Humanity is **NOT** something **'Out There'**.

It's about **All** of us **Collectively**
and was never more appropriate than

Right Here – Right Now!

– Jonathan Powell –

Start at THE BEGINNING

Know the FACTS

Anxiety is when a person experiences feeling of unease, worry or fear. When these feelings become persistent and begin impacting on daily life it could be a sign of an anxiety disorder such as, Generalised Anxiety Disorder (G.A.D.), which is a common type of anxiety disorder.

There is now growing evidence that some people may be more prone to anxiety and panic attacks than others and may have a genetic link or family predisposition. In addition, there is some research that points to the fact that some people may produce an excess of Adrenalin which may be closely linked to modern lifestyles, phobias and in particular diet.

With all the stresses and strains of modern living, panic attacks are commonplace for people from all walks of life and occur at almost at any age. They appear to be caused by several different situations including stress, sudden physical trauma, overwork, bereavement, accidents, and childbirth. This is often (but not always) characterised by a sudden onset of physical anxiety and hyperventilation often resulting from the body's natural human reaction to danger **'Fight or Flight'**.

This is a normal reaction to a situation whereby a person feels threatened or pressurised. Anxiety attacks can also be triggered by the association of previous experiences or events that have led to a previous attack. In addition, research into **Spontaneous Panic** attacks is thought to be related to chemical changes within the brain related to phobias and diet resulting in surges of adrenalin.

If you have ever experienced a panic attack you know how unpleasant it can be. They can often manifest very quickly, without apparent warning and feel incredibly intense. You feel anxious or fearful, your mouth feels dry and your heart feels like it is pounding.

Many people suffering from an attack will feel like their heart is giving out and may even think that they are going to die. But remember that whilst the experience is frightening the symptoms will only last a few minutes. The key is to take control.

As previously stated, the experience is an exaggeration of your body's normal reaction to stress. Thankfully, isolated panic attacks are mostly self-treatable. Often it is just a matter of learning to recognize those signs and symptoms and to understand what your body is doing. You can learn simple but effective techniques that help you release yourself from the crippling effects a panic attack can bring.

Though it feels like it lasts forever, a panic attack normally last between five and twenty minutes. While many people will only have one or two in their lifetime, if they should begin to happen on a regular basis (Four or more a month) and impede the day-to-day rhythm of your life, you may in fact have a **Panic Disorder**, which is less common. You should consult your Doctor for a full diagnosis.

Do persist in obtaining a complete diagnosis as people often suffer from symptoms of Panic disorder or Agoraphobia much longer than is necessary because of embarrassment or alternatively feel they are wasting their Doctor's time and should cope.

Without treatment, some forms of Agoraphobia can take several years to overcome. However, this condition can be successfully treated and allow sufferers to resume a normal life.

It is reportedly more common for women rather than men to suffer from **G.A.D.** (Generalised Anxiety Disorder) which may lead to panic attacks.[1] Left untreated, regular panic attacks can cripple and prevent people from living a 'normal' life. However thankfully panic attacks are very treatable, and you certainly don't need to suffer from them indefinitely.

What Are the Physical Signs?

If you've ever wondered about the power of our minds over our bodies, then a panic attack is an excellent example of just how powerful our thinking is over the mechanics of our bodies.

There are a range of physical symptoms that our mind can generate around our bodies. Of course, everyone is different, you may not personally endure all these symptoms to experience a full panic attack. However, if you have several of these together, it is likely you are having a panic attack.

* **Light headedness and/or dizziness.** This is often at the beginning of the attack. You can feel a little like you've had a few glasses too much to drink, or a sense the room is shifting a little around you. There may also be a rushing sound in your ears, as the blood moves away from your brain, causing you to feel like you may faint.

* **Difficulty in breathing.** Your mouth may go dry and your lips may have a tingling sensation. Your throat may feel as if it has a large lump in it, and it hurts to swallow. Your chest tightens and constricts and it's difficult to take deep slow breaths. If feels a little like you've just been sprinting for a few kilometres and you need to catch your breath.

* **Increased Heartrate.** Your pulse becomes faster and fluttery and sometimes a little uneven. Your heart is thumping against your chest and you seem unable to consciously slow it down even if you are sitting still.

* **Hot flushes.** Your face feels flushed and it feels almost as if you have a high temperature. You can also feel nauseous, as if you are trying to fight off an infection.

* **Waves of Anxiety.** The anxious feelings rise and fall through the attack as you struggle to regain control. As each wave comes it becomes a little more intense.

* **You feel Powerless.** Unable to prevent or influence unwanted and irrational thought processes. You feel unable to take control of your thoughts, you struggle to manipulate your thought direction. Your thoughts may skip from normal everyday concerns to imagined fears, often fantasizing the very worst outcome of whatever you are battling. It can run as a loop inside your mind, repeating the very thoughts you don't want or need.

* **Disconnected from reality.** You're unable to place the way you feel with what is happening. Often part of you will recognise that what you are thinking isn't normal, but you still can't stop it and it is so overwhelming. It's like there is two of you inside your head, one is stable and sensible while the other losing it! The irrational, fearful and panicking part of your mind overwhelms the normally logical sensible part.

* *Feeling out of control.* Panic/Severe Anxiety attacks are in the main, a loss of self-control. From the physical manifestation of panic through to your thought processes. You lose the ability to manage the way you think and act. The problem is that much of the effect is internal so while you may be deathly panicked on the inside, your heart is racing, and your mind is all over the place trying to logically justify what is happening. However, your physical body can appear calm and remain completely still. It's like panic is running a marathon inside your body, and you can't work out how it can escape.

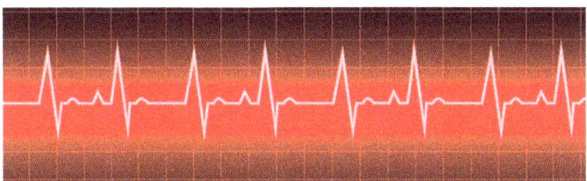

Many people confuse a panic attack with having a heart attack. The sensation can feel almost the same. Whilst this is unlikely, and you are at all concerned then it would be a good idea to seek out professional medical attention to ensure there is not a physical reason for your attack, particularly if you are in the 'At risk' category. If nothing else – it will give you peace of mind.

What Are the Symptoms?

Scientific researchers are still debating what specific conditions can cause panic attacks. However as stated previously, if other family members have suffered from them, there is a stronger likelihood that you may too. Stress and lifestyle of course can and does play a large factor with panic/anxiety attacks.

There are two types of 'Stress Hormones'[2] **Adrenalin** and **Cortisol (Hydrocortisone)** which act together to address the body's natural **'Fight or Flight'** response.

Adrenalin increases the heart and breathing rate, blood to clot faster and acts to draw blood away from your digestive tract whilst **Cortisol,** which is produced by the adrenalin glands, is designed to keep your response to the stressful situation going for as long as possible. It increases the blood sugars and counteracts the bodies normal production of Insulin. The trouble is too much of a good thing can produce the unpleasant symptoms of a panic/anxiety attack. Recent research[3] has shown that **Cortisol** levels may also differ for individuals with **Autism** or **Asperger's Syndrome**.

Often first appearing at times of great personal change. Stress factors such as getting married, having a child, moving homes, financial stress or changing career. Sudden changes that are out of your control such as the death of someone close to you, a marriage breakup or redundancy can also trigger a panic attack, particularly if there were additional stressors ongoing at the same time. There are also times when the cause of the attack is unclear or not immediately evident. This is not in itself a cause for concern (unless the episodes become frequent and sustained). The methods to overcome the anxiety attack remain the same.

If you have a close relative who suffers from depression or has been diagnosed as bipolar, that can also increase your chances of suffering from a panic attack.

However, as there are several physical ailments and conditions that can also share the same physical feelings as a panic attack. It is a very good idea to check as soon as possible that these are not causing your panic attacks.

Listed below, I have included some related medical conditions and terms that you may come across or hear about, possibly wondering and worrying what they are, and how they may specifically apply to you. My goal here is to give you a little knowledge and a greater understanding. Helping to repel any worries or fears you may have, either now or in the future.

* [Mitral Valve Prolapse (MVP)](#) – Symptoms are Heart Murmur.

This is when one of the heart valves (Flaps) does not close off properly. It is not a major condition but should be diagnosed and treated to prevent further complications. It is also known as Click-Murmur Syndrome or Barlow's Syndrome.

* [Tachycardia](#) – Medical term for a heart rate over 100 beats per minute.

Symptoms include, Chest Pain, Shortness of Breath, Rapid Pulse Rate, Heart Palpitations, Fainting and/or Light Headedness.

You may experience a raised heart rate due to a tachycardia attack. This may be a symptom of another heart related condition and a consultation with your doctor will probably suggest an ECG to check for any irregularities.

* Hyperthyroidism – Medical term for Overactive Thyroid.

Symptoms include, Palpitations, Sweating, Changes in menstrual patterns, Mood changes, Excessive bowel movements, Tremors in hands and fingers, Difficulty in sleeping, Fatigue/Muscle weakness and increased appetite.

This is also often accompanied with an unintentional loss of weight even though the appetite and food intake remain the same or increases. This condition can be serious if ignored. Fortunately, this can be checked with a simple blood test and is treatable.

* Hypoglycaemia – Low Blood Sugar *(Glucose)* levels usually but not exclusively associated with **Diabetes**.

Symptoms include, Fatigue, Anxiety, Tingling of the lips, tongue or cheeks, Sweating, Hunger, Shakiness, Irritability, Pale skin and an irregular or fast heartbeat.

Glucose is the body's primary energy source. A very low blood sugar count can send your body into overdrive as it tries to protect the brain and keeps it functioning. This can also be a precursor to **Diabetes**. A test of your **glucose** tolerance can help earmark whether this could be an issue for you. It can last from a few days to several weeks and can be self-treated. However, severe cases should be referred to your Doctor.

* Stimulant Use Disorder – Substance misuse leading to behavioural issues and potential addiction.

Symptoms/Characteristics include, Dilated Pupils, Rapid Heart Rate, Hyperactivity, weight loss, sweating, Stealing, Deceit (Lying) using excessive amounts of prescription drugs, irrational behaviour, and anxiety / nervousness.

The overuse of any stimulant/substance that artificially increases the heart rate. Ranging from prescription drugs for ADHD and amphetamines to illegal drugs such as Cocaine.

Excessive consumption of coffees and energy drinks which include Caffeine can also display some of the symptoms and characteristics shown above.

Prescription Drugs and Change of Medication

You should always be aware that any new medicine and/or tablets that has been prescribed by your Doctor, is producing the normal expected result. If this is not the case and you experience any unexpected side effect(s), then check the enclosed accompanied documentation which will usually include a section on 'Known Side Effect's. (The Side Effect may well be a harmless temporary condition). If not or the documentation is unavailable and you believe there is cause for concern then, contact your Doctor or Pharmacist at the earliest opportunity.

When stopping medication that you have been taking for a considerable time, sometimes this can result in a physical reaction as your brain adjusts to the different chemicals in your body.

If you have been on a specific course of drugs (Normally 3 weeks or more) i.e., Steroids then you **must consult your Doctor before you stop taking them**. It is important to gradually reduce the dose over a given period. These types of drugs replace the body's ability to produce certain functions and sudden withdrawal may cause a sharp fall in blood pressure and affect the blood sugar levels. In addition, it could potentially lead to failure of the Adrenal Gland which produces vital hormones for the body. Such sudden withdrawal can also result in the return of the symptoms for which it was originally prescribed (Swelling, inflammation, Blood conditions etc.)

A consultation with you Doctor will render suggestions on how to provide your body with the best way to have little or indeed no reaction to the withdrawal.

* Hormone Imbalance[4] – The Body's Chemical Imbalance.

Produced in the Endocrine Glands, Hormones are chemical messengers that control the body's major processes including metabolism and reproduction etc. Tiny changes can have serious effects throughout our whole body.

Hormonal Balance can be changed in many ways. Some are caused naturally, for instance by puberty and the menopause. Others can be directly affected by lifestyle or toxins.

The bodies levels of **glucose** are produced by the hormone **cortisol**, dependant on its needs. High stress levels may lead to excessive demands on the production of **cortisol** which can lead to **Hyperadrenia** (Adrenalin Fatigue). The symptoms of which can trigger panic attacks. Adrenalin fatigue is a growing problem today and can lead to **Hyperthyroidism** and other complications if left untreated.

A healthy and well-balanced diet is crucial for hormonal health. Reduce consumption of heavily processed foods, especially those containing refined sugars. Balance your meals with a varied and wholesome diet.

Avoid over processed foods and re-processed meat, eat oily fish, and use organic foods with plenty of fruits and vegetables. This will greatly improve your overall health, including the regulation of hormone production.

Anxiety and Depression

Depression is never a trivial condition and is so much more than simply feeling unhappy or feeling down for a few days. Bouts of depression can last for long periods of time and can lead to many physical and emotional issues from Weight Loss and Insomnia to Anxiety Disorders and Mental Health problems.

It's perfectly normal to feel anxious or depressed occasionally, especially in response to life's stressors. However, when these feelings become prolonged, disproportionate, or apparent, for little or no significant reason, they should always be addressed.

Thankfully, diagnosis and treatment methods have come a long way in recent years, with many organizations, public health services and individuals (including celebrities) coming together to bring mental illness to the forefront of public awareness.

The combination of anxiety and depression is a recognized feature of anxiety disorders. Whilst behavioral and emotional symptoms may differ within the two, the fact remains they are both an undesirable and unwelcome state of mental health.

Represented by a consistent and overwhelming state of fear or worry, anxiety can be difficult and laborious in its physical manifestations too. The symptoms of depression may be similar with unrelenting feelings of sadness or despair.

Precise explanations arising to this condition remain unclear, as its effects differ from person to person. However, changes in brain chemistry, genetic factors, and hormone function are all believed to play a role. Irrespective of the cause, mental illness requires and generally responds well to professional treatment.

Depression can also bring on panic attacks. It's important to look at the whole range of feelings and symptoms you are dealing with. Whilst it is possible to alter your behaviour, and learn simple methods to cope, it is equally as important to ensure you receive the correct professional guidance and medication (when required) to help you, allowing you to concentrate on learning the coping strategies and methods that suit your situation.

Methods of Treating Anxiety and Depression

Whilst our understanding of mental illness has progressively evolved over time, it still can present certain difficulties. Diagnostically speaking, depression and anxiety fundamentally affects the behaviour of an individual, how they feel and think. Therefore, we generally rely upon them to identify these changes themselves and seek the appropriate help.

In some cases, family members or close friends may be able to identify vulnerable individuals and assist them in requesting attention. Once diagnosed, treatment can be quite successful using a variety of different approaches, the most common of which are psychological therapies or 'talking therapies'.

Such therapies are generally administered by a qualified psychologist and involve either behaviour modification (Cognitive Behavior Therapy or CBT) or an examination of intrapersonal (Thought Processes) and interpersonal (Relationship/Communicational) patterns and behaviours.

The aim of these therapies is to identify and address the key 'triggers' and focus upon methods of managing future events. Such therapies are often combined with improving nutrition and encouraging regular exercise, which can actively promote a healthy mental state.

Focus on nutrition is the first step towards self-empowerment and taking control over one's diet. Safe and effective, the benefits are both psychological and physiological. Helping to Reduce or eliminate spikes caused by sugar-laden foods and stimulants, such as excess coffee, cigarettes, etc., and will help in reducing the debilitating feelings associated with general anxiety.

Children and Young Adults Can be Affected

Young people and children are unfortunately just as vulnerable to mental illnesses such as anxiety and depression. While it is often more difficult and harder to detect, professionally diagnosed and applied therapies for children and juveniles, can assist them substantially towards living a happier and more fulfilling childhood.

A happier childhood prepares the child better for dealing with the stresses of the teenage years and young adulthood. Providing a healthy and safe transition to young adulthood enables the individual to prepare for a life of being in control and empowered to deal with the everyday challenges that test us all.

Hopefully, after exploring all other options, the use of antidepressant medication may be required and prescribed accordingly. This will of course depend on the severity of the illness and is most often used in conjunction with psychotherapies. Antidepressants can be very effective in certain situations. Treatment will normally be specifically tailored to suit the individual, based upon a thorough study of their personal history of symptoms, responses, and their environment.

Finally, one of the results of over anxiety and depression in juveniles and young children is anger. Often directed towards those that are closest to them such as parents, siblings, or friends. You should consider seeking professional advice in dealing with situation, particularly if the child is undergoing treatment in the form of counselling or therapy. Your well-being and health are paramount in allowing you to cope and ultimately be in the best position to help the child.

ANGER is a normal and useful emotion but can become a problem if the behaviour becomes out of control or aggressive. Tackle the issue *together* – Let them know that you are empathetic. Encourage them to recognize the early signs, calmly discuss the 'triggers' and the potential results. Help them to overcome the problem by giving the anger a name or picture (which they can draw). Strategies on what action they can take to avoid the episodes such as Walking away from the situation, breathing slowly and deeply or quietly talking to someone they trust. Most importantly be a team, act together! It is in both your interests.

What Causes a Panic Attack?

In many ways our bodies are perfectly designed to do what they should, but in the modern world in which we live today, our bodies do not have the same evolutionary stress requirements as having to outrun a hungry sabre-toothed tiger. As previously stated, our natural defence system against stress is our **'fight or flight'** response which is one of our most primitive behavioural instinctive responses. It is also one of the most powerful. It is meant to be *extremely* powerful, as it's designed to ensure our survival and protect us from unexpected danger such as falling trees, fast moving traffic and anything else that may come between us and life. This instinctive response speeds up your heart, pumps adrenaline into your bloodstream and prepares you to run for your life. Our bodies have not evolved to cope with the modern world we live in, so whilst our brain is telling us to run, our bodies remain still.

The **'fight or flight'** response is meant to help us either stand and cope with the danger or run away from it. It's normal and it's natural. What makes a panic attack different is there is no physical danger – it's just the expectation or pre-emptive possibility of danger that's triggering it. This situation may not be evident or apparent to you or an onlooker. While some panic attacks can be attributed to a family history of panic attacks, or to a psychological disorder, they can also occur with no clear reason.

Remembering that you will survive, and the attack will pass, is perhaps the first step in conquering the attacks and learning how to manage them.

How to Confront a Panic Attack
First things first!

Know this and **commit this to memory.** Whilst what you are experiencing is very disturbing and frightening the symptoms are **NOT** dangerous or harmful! – this experience is a literal exaggeration of your body's normal reaction to stress. Although it may appear to last longer, attacks rarely last more than 5-20 minutes.

Try to avoid resisting the feelings, the sooner you face the situation the quicker the experiences will subside and the less intense they will become. Try to stay focused and accept the situation.

Xscape Anxiety

Breathing Exercise

Slowly inhale deeply (filling your chest) and exhale fully, repeat this 2-3 times. Try to label your level of fear from 1-10 and then try counting backwards from 100. You will inevitably become aware that as you count back the level of perceived fear will also lessen.

Over breathing (hyperventilation) can cause symptom of numbness and tingling of the hands, and dizziness. This results in lowering the carbon dioxide levels (CO2) in the blood. Try to concentrate on your breathing, hold on to the last breath you took and let the oxygen in your body move to the place it should be. if you can do this once or twice for ten to fifteen seconds it should help you. Continue with this breathing exercise above. Alternatively, locate a paper bag,* place it over your mouth, then slowly breath in and out into it. This re-breathing your own carbon dioxide helps to correct the blood acid level **(pCO2)** that had been upset by over-breathing.

If possible, go for a walk or even a gentle run. Exercise makes your heart rate go up and you will be using up all the adrenaline too. Regular exercise also helps to reduce stress levels overall.

Once all the symptoms have cleared, congratulate yourself on your achievement and remember how you did it. In the unlikely event that you should get a re-occurrence then you will know how to overcome it even quicker.

If you are still at all concerned about the attack or are worried about any underlying causes, then do make an appointment to see your Doctor. They will be happy to provide a check-up and advise you accordingly.

The Doctor may (dependant on their initial prognosis) advise having some blood tests done. This would rule out such things as Diabetes, Thyroid problems etc… They may also consider an

ECG (Electrocardiogram) test to check that your heart is operating normally.

It would also be a good idea to get your eyes checked as this may be the cause of 'dizzy spells' or headaches.

If a physical condition is found to exist which is contributing to the attacks, then treatment can be made, and the attacks will inevitably stop.

Not everyone that suffers a Panic or Anxiety attack is stressed, overworked, tired, anxious, or suffering traumatic events. Panic attacks are known to run in families and can strike at anyone at any time.

Unconditional acceptance is the first and major step for overcoming the condition and leading a normal life. Do examine your personality – Do you have any traits that lead to states of High Anxiety? If the answer is **"Yes"** then I would recommend the services of a trained therapist to help and guide you to use these traits positively.

Be honest with yourself and take a close look at your lifestyle and make changes that will help you in the long term. If you feel that your judgment is a little suspect, then get trusted friends or family to comment on your lifestyle. Simple changes like exercise, diet and mental attitude can make huge differences to your quality of life and have a massive effect any adverse symptoms you experience.

---

* Asthmatics and those previously diagnosed with existing bronchial/cardiac conditions are cautioned to use this method under medical guidance only.

Carers Note:

You must be empathetic with the sufferer. Let them within reason set their pace of recovery. Don't unwittingly set 'tests' or appear confrontational by saying things like **"Pull yourself together"**, **"Relax"** or **"Calm down"**; what the person is experiencing is very real and traumatic to them.

It is quite normal for <u>you</u> to feel concerned or anxious, but do not become overdramatic yourself. Try not to allow avoidance of the situation, encourage them to take deep and slow breaths.

Be positive and patient, providing plenty of encouragement – **"Well Done"**.

You set yourself up to succeed when you learn to focus on what you can accomplish in a day.

Anxiety / Panic Disorder is the next level of an isolated panic attack. This is normally diagnosed if the sufferer is experiencing four or more attacks within a month with fears of another impending attack.

If you are aware that this is possibly the case with the person you are with, then you should refer them to their Doctor at the earliest convenience. Whilst the symptoms are rarely more frightening or harmful than isolated attacks, the long-term effects can be extremely negative for the sufferer and they may not be able to function properly at work or home resulting in poor relationships and quality of life.

Modern Day Stress Can Trigger Panic Attacks...

It has previously been accepted that people who live high powered, stressful lives such as Senior Company Executives, Medical Staff, and Celebrities etc… were more likely to suffer from anxiety attacks. However, within our modern world today almost anyone regardless of age, sex or position can suffer with them.

Most adults today are required to work, (increasingly within an ever diminishing and insecure workplace) to maintain their financial commitments. The times of your partner 'staying at home to bring up the family' are sadly diminished. Students also, are required to meet ever increasing expectations with raised standards of education and associated costs. Social pressures now pervade all aspects of our modern life.

Longer working days

We put pressure on ourselves to meet all targets and to work any extra hours required when needed, this is creating extra stress in our everyday lives.

Wanting to better ourselves

More people now want to further their education be it through university, online courses, or adult education. All this expectation and stress can add to the panic triggers within you.

In addition, our rapidly changing cultures now place hitherto unknown pressures on civilization today. These include relatively instant worldwide communication, such as the mobile phone, Satellite television and personal IT equipment (World Wide Web). Instead of just being affected by local or national events we are now part of a global community. All of which exposes us to the latest news which is frequently bad. Whether it's environmental, a financial crises or tragic loss of lives. This can have a negative and pessimistic effect on our lives. Of course, conversely good news can have a positive and optimistic effect. The trouble is there is seemingly never enough good news and its certainly true that bad news takes priority.

Information Technology has brought us huge benefits globally, but conversely has also placed additional stresses on our modern civilization. For example, Media exposure of crime statistics and localised terrorism creates a fear culture with adults who as a result, experience the need to protect their offspring. No longer encouraging their children to play outside or go and explore open spaces (As in previous decades) unless it is visiting a predestined place or organised venue. Many young people tend to spend most of their time within the confines of their (or friends) homes watching TV, playing on Games machines or on the computer. They in turn (Often due to peer pressure) would not willingly venture outside their immediate areas. The 'Social Media' platforms have also had a significant effect on the lifestyles and expectations of people today.

As the stress in our lives expands the pressure increases. It's a little like one of those whistling kettles that explode with steam and noise once they get to the right temperature. The pressure builds and builds until there is nowhere for it to go but course through your body. The more stress you place on your body and mind every day, the closer you are to that boiling point.

The human brain has evolved over millennia to ensure our survival. It is constantly checking and rechecking to make sure we have all the reactions and chemicals we need to safely live our lives. It is always ready to kick start our **'fight or flight'** response, ready to protect us against whatever is our enemy. It can't tell the difference between a metaphorical imagined danger, or a real sabre-toothed tiger. To all intents and purposes, the former is just as dangerous, and we need protecting from it. The panic attack is merely our body's way of trying to look after us the way our bodies have been caring for us since we first experienced stress millennia ago.

Just because our brain thinks its life threatening doesn't mean that it is. It just means our most primitive part of our body, the part that works completely on instinct rather than logic or reason has decided we need a bit of a kick start. This can be either because we're living on a constant rollercoaster of stress or because something in our environment has reminded us of something we associate with danger and the need for a **fight** or **flight** reaction. If you've ever brushed past a car alarm, barely touching it and it's gone off then you'll know how easy it can be to set off something incredibly sensitive. Our **'fight or flight'** response can be like that too. We can become so sensitive that it starts up at the smallest incident and it's difficult to stop it once its screams of protest of impending danger have begun.

Alleviating Fears of Anxiety/Panic Attacks

The solution to alleviating these fears is straightforward. If we go to the example of the whistling kettle, the simplest way to stop it boiling and reduce all that steam and noise is to **turn down the heat!**

Attacks can be managed or prevented in the same way. All we need do is to turn down the heat by relieving the stress that has built up. Even if the day-to-day stress remains, we can learn to manage it at a simmering boil, rather than at a fast and furious pace.

Anxiety/Panic attacks can feel like a very personal and private terror. Externally it can appear that everything is perfectly fine, whilst internally we are feeling very frightened and confused. Many people suffering from attacks can also feel they are isolated and set apart from others. However, the problem is reasonably common and widespread. Many people have suffered from them, and large numbers of those have successfully found methods to reduce or eradicate the attacks entirely.

There are some common assumptions and beliefs about panic attacks that sufferers hold. Perhaps you may have experienced some of these for yourself.

It's going to make your heart give out, and you'll die!

Regardless of how hard your heart appears to be pounding in your chest, it is far stronger than you give it credit for. It is the strongest muscle in our bodies and perfectly designed to be able to take a rapid increase- just as it would if you were running a marathon or doing a funky dance class. If you are at all concerned that you may have a heart condition, it would be wise to get it checked out, if only to provide you with peace of mind. However, for most people, our hearts will be completely fine during and after an attack.

You won't get enough air to your lungs!

Many people find it hard to breathe properly during a panic attack. However, you are taking in more air than you imagine. The tightness and accompanying lightness of breath is caused by **hyperventilation**, with your breathing causing an excess of oxygen to move throughout your body.

You may faint!

It is highly unlikely that you will faint because your body is programmed to protect you from any perceived danger. If it was a physical threat your body would want to keep you upright and moving quickly away from danger. Even if your danger isn't a physical one, your body is increasing your consciousness and you are incredibly alert. If worst comes to worst and you did faint, think of the benefits. At least you'd have some rest from the thumping in your chest if you did faint. The sense that you might faint comes from a condition known as **hyperventilation**. Even though you may feel weak and as if you are going to faint, your large muscles are soaking in oxygen and are pumped and ready for action.

You are having a stroke!

Because your body is experiencing a wide range of sensations It is quite normal to try and work out what is causing it. However, all the physical sensations are very unlikely to be from a deeper issue such as a stroke. Your body isn't about to self-destruct. It's just doing a very natural thing in a time of extreme stress.

Remember a rapid way of telling if someone is suffering from a stroke is to remember the acronym **F.A.S.T**. which requires an assessment of three specific symptoms of stroke.

Facial weakness?

Can the person smile? Has their mouth or eye drooped?

Arm weakness?

Can the person raise both arms?

Speech problems?

Can the person speak clearly and understand what you say?

Time to

Call the Emergency Services!

You feel as though you are going crazy!

As a result of feeling you are not in control, the whole experience may cause you to think that you are losing your mind and/or abstract from the situation. However, all that is happening is that your body is reacting to the need to escape the situation you've found yourself in. You are still in control, it's just a different part of your brain that is organizing your body. Your body is allowing your subconscious mind to take precedence. Those thought processes are a very logical and sane solution to your needs.

You are going to embarrass yourself!

It is human nature to be worried or concerned when we personally experience a loss of control, either physical or mentally. Whether it is being sick or unwell in a public area, displaying unwanted emotions at an inappropriate time or place, or simply just having uncomfortable thought processes. It is something we all have in common!

Fortunately, it is also normal behaviour for most people to show empathy and compassion to others, (even strangers!). i.e., anyone that has hurt themselves, someone crying or distressed, or showing signs of Ill-health are likely to be shown kindness and offered help. So, try not to be over-concerned, whilst it certainly is an uncomfortable situation for anyone to be in, you should do your best to completely **accept the situation** and seek the help you need at that point. Remember – **It will pass!**

In conclusion, remember that while you feel like everyone can see how you are feeling; most of what you are experiencing isn't noticeable to anyone else. As previously stated, Anxiety/Panic attacks are very personal things. What key factors trigger one person to have an attack can be very different to those of other people. Most panic attacks last no longer than a few minutes. So, accept the situation, it will pass, and life will resume to normality. You can then begin to calmly address the issues that led to the episode.

Understanding Fear

Phobias

Phobias are fear-based reactions to something that appears irrational in nature and can lead to panic attacks. There is no scientific reason to feel fearful, as it is possible to overcome whatever the causes of a particular phobia are. That is not to say that some phobias aren't based on the potential for real harm, but realistically you are unlikely to face any physical danger other than the emotional stress and anxiety caused when the phobia presents itself. Let's look at some of the most common phobias and how to deal with them.

Common Phobias

* Social Phobia – Also known as social anxiety disorder, this is a phobia that can affect everyone differently. One person might only be afraid of speaking in front of people, while another person fears just chatting at the dinner table. The main thing that really affects someone with a social anxiety disorder is the fear of panic attacks. It literally causes someone to feel as if they are dying when going out, being around others, and interacting with them.

* Anthropophobia – This is different from social anxiety because the fear of people manifests as fear of even

people they know. People who have this fear are terrified of everyone, **not just people they do not know**

* Aerophobia – The fear of flying is a common phobia. Some people can fly through their fears, but others cannot and need to find alternative transportation. This fear can be very limiting if someone wants to experience a new type of life or career that requires traveling.

* Mysophobia – A common phobia is the fear of germs. Due to this fear, it may be hard for the person to go out around people. They may be afraid to touch others or touch surfaces, and it might manifest as keeping a home spotlessly clean and overly washing the hands, which (ironically) can end up causing skin infections.

* Glossophobia – A common phobia whereby people are so fearful of public speaking that they often describe it as scarier than death. While some people simply suffer from some stage fright and can get through it, a person with this phobia will avoid public speaking at all costs. This can damage their grades in school and career later in life.

* Arachnophobia – A very common phobia, which is the fear of spiders, other arachnids and scorpions. Whereby the person will be terrified and will make every possible effort to distance themselves away from them. As with most phobias overcoming the fear is most often successful when there is a controlled program of confrontation to the fear. Beginning with handing images and toys through to gradual exposure the phobia.

* Agoraphobia – Perhaps one of the most debilitating of phobias. Agoraphobia is one of the most complex of phobias and is closely associated with anxiety/panic attacks. A person suffering from this condition fears leaving the confines of their home and will take extreme measures to remain within their comfort zone. It is covered here in more detail in the following chapter.

* Acrophobia – The fear of heights, also a reasonably common phobia whereby the person has an extreme and irrational fear of being up high, even if they are not particularly high. This phobia belongs to a category of specific phobias called **'Space and Motion Discomfort'**. This condition obviously prevents participation in certain careers as well as lifestyle choices such as specific hobbies and sports.

How to Deal with Phobias

To overcome your phobias, the first step you need to take is to identify the specific phobia /fear and then be able to make a judgement as to what level it affects your life and well-being. The best course of action is to seek professional medical help and guidance in overcoming the phobia.

Alternatively, another way would be truly acknowledging the phobia and its effects. Plan to determinedly work through the fear a little each day. Keep a journal/workbook so that you can record your actions and subsequent results. This will enable you to develop your approach plans to push through the fear of this phobia one step at a time. Remember your goal and if you should fail then you can always try again later or seek available help.

You may also consider hypnotherapy, psychotherapy, or even a life coach who specializes in your phobia. Whatever method you choose to use, you should remember that phobias are not impossible to overcome, if you have the desire and willingness to try and do what the professionals advise – such as desensitization, neuro-linguistic programming and any prescribed medications that may help.

When it's Agoraphobia

Agoraphobia is an anxiety disorder that becomes an issue when a person suffering from repeated anxiety attacks consistently worries about having one in a public place. Whereby, they are unable to hide the effects from others. Particularly if it's in a place, they cannot easily extract themselves from or get help if needed. They become desperate to avoid being noticed. Approximately thirty percent of anxiety/panic attack sufferers develop **agoraphobia**.

Left untreated anxiety/panic attacks occurring on a regular basis can develop into **agoraphobia.** It's one of the reasons why it is a good idea to seek treatment as early as possible.

Are you at risk of developing **agoraphobia**? If you have experienced some of the following symptoms, it is advisable to go have a chat to your doctor about whether **agoraphobia** may be a potential problem for you.

Agoraphobics are afraid of the following:

* Being in an open place. You feel exposed and vulnerable when you don't have clearly defined physical boundaries.

* Entering public places, going shopping or being part of a crowd. It can almost feel the adverse of **agoraphobic** with a sense that everything is closing in and feeling stifling. Escape is the only thing you want.

* Traveling in planes, buses, and trains where you are part of a crowd.

* Being in a lift or on a bridge. Anything, that cannot be escaped from easily.

* A café, movie theatre or restaurant that you cannot walk out of whenever you want to.

* Any location that is unfamiliar and different. Many agoraphobics become virtual recluses, preferring to stay at home where everything is perceived to be more easily controlled.

Obsessive-Compulsive Disorder (OCD)

People who suffer from anxiety attacks can also develop other phobias or **Obsessive-Compulsive Disorder (OCD)** complex which is usually split into two broad types of namely **Obsession** and **Compulsion**. Many sufferers display symptoms of both obsession and compulsion but usually lean more toward one than the other.

There are several different types of **OCD** including obsessive thoughts and compulsions such as checking, washing / cleaning, placing close attention to order and hoarding.

Many experiencing **OCD** can and do suffer from more than one symptom simultaneously which is why the complaint causes so much distress and anxiety to them and those closest to them.

This condition mainly affects people in the 18-35 age range and can last several years or even be lifelong. Urgent professional guidance and treatment is strongly advised. As in the case of anxiety/panic attacks there can be a genetic disposition. Professional diagnosis is normally carried out after a laboratory test.

These fears develop when your mind naturally wants to avoid those foods or types of exercise or behaviours that you believe may be triggering your anxiety attacks. This in turn creates a greater likelihood of further attacks if you are confronted with these stimuli.

Compulsions

Checking

This type of **OCD** involves repeatedly checking things. For Example, making sure that doors and windows are locked, switches are turned off and daily tasks are completed. This often involves many trips backwards and forwards to ensure the checking has definitely taken place. This type of behaviour often stems from the fear that something bad will happen if it is not done, sometimes being traced backed to childhood. Increasingly, complicated daily checking; rituals of this type can take up significant amounts of time as well as having a disruptive effect on day-to-day life.

Washing and Cleaning

This type of **OCD** involves repeated washing of the hands, cleaning clothes and housework. It is often based around the fear of being contaminated by dirt and germs. Despite washing hands, clothes and cleaning the same things at least several times a day, the fear of contamination remains. Sufferers will often go to extreme lengths to avoid contact with situations they feel will expose them to dirt and germs.

Ordering

This type of **OCD** involves an almost irrational desire to place things in order. For example, Dispenser Tins of Tea, Sugar and Coffee must be stored in that order or cold drinks must be lined up with the label forward on the top shelf of the refrigerator (And only on the top). If the object is not in the desired position, then it can cause considerable distress to the sufferer and they may spend considerable amounts of time ensuring things are in the 'correct' or 'perfect' order.

Obsessions

This type of **OCD** constantly is thinking negative thoughts and images, often relating to self-harm and the harming of others. These thoughts and images will often flash into the mind without warning and cause sufferers to become very distressed. To detract from the unwelcome intrusions, sufferers often revert to repetition such as praying, silent counting, chanting or silent repetition of certain words or phrases.

Hoarding

Whilst most people have no problems when it comes to getting rid of excess clutter that is not required or wanted. This type of **OCD** involves the inability to throw anything out, including items that are insignificant and of no real value. This often results in an untidy environment that is challenging to live in or with.

Although there are other types of **OCD** patients are not restricted to symptoms that fit these main types. Experts suggest that these are the main types that most **OCD** sufferers will experience. Most patients tending to endure symptoms of at least two types of **OCD** at any one time, although this is not universal. Many people with **OCD** will go out of their way to avoid situations that create stress in a bid to limit its symptoms. This is particularly common for students with **OCD**.

Avoiding Stressful Situations

For some **OCD** sufferers, avoiding stressful situations is enough to keep their **OCD** under control (particularly in association with therapy and medication). It makes sense to avoid certain situations as an anti-stress strategy and endeavour to decrease the intensity of symptoms. This is a good idea in theory, particularly if your **OCD** is intensified by specific situations.

However, avoiding stressful situations may not always be possible. For example, many young adults first develop **OCD** when attending university away from the family home and familiar surroundings. In this situation, a student with **OCD** cannot feasibly avoid the lectures or seminars that may contribute to their stress and anxiety.

Cognitive Behaviour Therapy (CBT)
Breaking the Hold

While avoiding situations that are known to cause stress and worsen the symptoms of **OCD**, you may want to confront your fears, especially if you are dramatically compromising yourself to avoid stressful situations.

One of the treatments for **OCD** is **Cognitive Behaviour Therapy (CBT)**, which involves directly addressing the hold that **OCD** has on sufferers. For example, if you have a recurrent compulsion to clean and wash your hands because of fear of contamination, **CBT** will force you to tackle this head-on by not allowing you to wash your hands immediately after touching an object that you are afraid is contaminated.

Treatment for **CBT** involves talking and counselling and has proven successful for approximately 50% of those suffering from panic attacks or **agoraphobia**. The therapy works because it helps to give the sufferer an understanding of what thoughts and emotions, they are likely to experience, prior to a panic attack. This then allows the sufferer to modify their future behaviours and therefore lessen the impact of any impending attack (or avoid it altogether). **CBT** is based upon the premise that the way we think and process our thoughts can as a trigger for our attacks. The resulting loop (repeated thoughts, such as *"I can't deal with ..."*) is examined and tackled head on. Wanting to avoid certain situations as an anti-stress mechanism is not uncommon for **OCD** sufferers, particularly for students. This tends to have a big effect on everyday life, particularly if they feel they must go to extreme lengths to avoid potentially stressful situations.

Taking Control

If you make a conscious effort to avoid potentially stressful situations for fear of aggravating your **OCD** symptoms, **CBT** will provide the tools to help you deal with avoidance issues. The therapist will encourage you to confront your fears, guiding you through those scenarios that normally trigger an attack, giving you the confidence to take control of the situation. This is intended to educate your mind so that you no longer feel the need to avoid stressful situations on the off chance that they may make your **OCD** symptoms worse.

For most **OCD** sufferers, venturing into the potentially stressful situations that they would normally avoid is far from an easy process, and can cause varying levels of distress and anxiety (particularly if it is initially unsuccessful). However, if you are keen to prevent **OCD** from taking over your life completely then **CBT** may be a good idea in the long term. It can potentially take a long time to achieve the desired results, but many **OCD** sufferers are eventually able to break the hold at least partially if not completely. This is rarely an overnight process and much patience is needed. Treatment may also be used alongside Mantras, Breathing techniques or Yoga.

Compose a Mantra

Devise an affirmation — a short, clear, positive statement that focuses on your coping abilities.

Dr. Elkin says,

"Affirmations are a good way to silence the self-critical voice we all carry with us that only adds to our stress".

The next time you feel as if your life is one disaster after another, repeat 10 times,

"I feel calm. I can handle this."

'You should never view
your challenges as a disadvantage.
Instead, it's important for you to
understand that your experience facing
and overcoming adversity is actually one
of your biggest advantages.'

- Michelle Obama

Mental Health and Wellbeing

Anger Management

The emotion of anger, (including feelings of rage and frustration) may appear to be unrelated to the symptoms of anxiety disorders and panic attacks. They are in fact normal biological responses to **'Fight'** or **'Flight'** situations and incidents. Humans and other mammals are programmed physically and biologically to re-act accordingly. The **'Fight'** or **'Flight'** mechanism is at work deep within our psyche and often two sides of the same coin. Heart rate is increased, breathing is deeper and faster, blood pressure climbs significantly, insulin production within our body is increased, even the blood flow is increased to our limbs like the arms and hands in preparation for a fight. It is how we handle it that can become a problem, both to ourselves and those around us.

Continued suppression of episodes of anger leads to stress and then conversely, the stress can lead to further episodes of anger. It can become a vicious circle if we allow the situation to get out of control. We are putting ourselves at serious risk of long-term health and social problems.

Anger is a positive and useful emotion if it is expressed appropriately. However, the long-term physical effects of uncontrolled or supressed anger include increased anxiety, high blood pressure and headache, which are often caused by chemical imbalances in the brain. This involves the imbalance of neurotransmitters in the brain. These neurotransmitters in the brain are the catalytic signals between neurons and atoms.

There are several signs of chemical imbalances of the brain, including increased hormone stress levels, increased levels of toxic neurochemicals and limited neurotransmitters. Stress is commonly linked to chemical imbalances of the brain. This sign is often fuelled by an individual's increased stress level.

Self-recognition of the problem is paramount to alleviate this unpleasant experience. Discuss it with those who are most likely to be affected i.e., loved ones, friends, and work colleagues. Create a support network of those who care about you. Seek help and advice of your doctor who will advise you on long-term strategies for anger management including regular physical exercise, learning relaxation techniques and counselling.

Healthy Ways to Vent Frustration

We all can get angry and frustrated. It's a natural part of life, and it's okay to feel exasperated sometimes. The problem isn't with the emotion itself. The problem is in how you express it.

In the past, therapists used to prescribe what they referred to as 'benign behaviour.' These are things like punching your pillow, screaming at the top of your lungs, or throwing your old stuff from the edge of a cliff. They described it as being cathartic.

While that may be true, in a sense, the fear is allowing it to escalate to more intense types of behaviour. This usually happens in the heat of the moment when your rage cripples your logical thinking. What starts as 'benign' can cause harm to yourself or others.

The great author, Isak Dinesen, said,

"The cure for anything is salt water: sweat, tears, or the sea."

Below are a few suggestions to help alleviate your frustration and anger. Whilst some of these you will be able to do on your own, others you'll need the help of a good support buddy.

Cry

Research shows that crying is a positive and healthy way to let off steam. You release pent-up negative energy by relieving your body of stress-inducing hormones.

The reason? When you cry, you activate the parasympathetic division of your nervous system. As a result, your heart rate decreases, along with your blood pressure. Plus, it reduces stress and helps restore your body's state of balance.

Another reason why crying is good for you is **Manganese**. This mood-regulating chemical helps combat and anxiety and depression.

Write

You don't have to be a trained therapist to know that writing your feelings down on paper is therapeutic. When they're in front of you, these negative emotions become tangible, they're not just some random thoughts floating in your brain anymore.

Keep a journal/diary to record your daily life including those instances of emotional episodes that you faced and how you re-acted to them. Over a short period of time, you will notice and be able to identify those events and situations that have triggered your unwanted reactions and most importantly what has been successful for **you** in overcoming them.

Once you create some space between you and your anger, it gives you a fresh perspective of the situation. Giving you clarity of thought. You become in control of your feelings, and not the other way around.

Some people take an alternative approach, by writing their thoughts and feelings on a piece of paper, <u>then tearing it up</u>. Whilst others will throw their paper into their fireplace and <u>watch it burn</u>, thereby like a cleansing ritual, disposing of their unwanted thoughts and feelings in a demonstrable way!

Try all three techniques and see which one works for you.

Exercise

This is one of the best ways to vent your frustration. The best part is that it can be as simple as taking a walk or as hardcore as climbing a mountain. It's up to you!

Exercise is good therapy for several reasons. One, it releases endorphins. These 'feel-good' hormones are responsible for reducing anger and stress. They also enhance your mood, boost your concentration levels, and improve the quality of your sleep.

On top of all that, you burn calories and build some muscles. By looking and feeling terrific, your self-confidence will improve.

To get even more out of your workout, pick a physical activity you can do outdoors. You can jog, hike, take a walk—whatever feels comfortable to you. If you live near the beach, go for a swim, as Dinesen suggests, and let the saltwater wash away your frustrations.

The point is to connect with nature and smell some fresh air. It'll remind you to focus more on the bigger picture and that there's more to life. You may even realize that what's been bothering you isn't as big as you had imagined.

Meditate

If you're a parent, you're probably already quite an expert on the quick 10-second version. When you're confronting your child and their argument is getting to you, what do you do? – you take a deep breath, close your eyes, and slowly count to 10.

That's meditating! A condensed form of it, but it works just the same.

The great thing about meditation is that you can do it anywhere, at any time, and for however long you want. You can also enhance the mood by lighting a scented candle or listening to some ambient sounds such as rain falling, a river flowing, or waves crashing on the shore. Some people prefer to have a relaxing 'white noise' in the background, whilst others to sit somewhere completely quiet in isolation with no distractions of any kind.

Better still get away from the situation and try to visualize a peaceful place or relaxing experience. Close your eyes and imagine you are there in your mind. Make it your personal haven.

The one thing that remains constant in all forms of meditation is your breathing.

Breathe

Try some "new and improved" variations of counting to ten. For instance, try counting to ten with a deep slow breath in between each number or pacing the numbers with **"one numpty, two numpties, three numpties, four"** etc. Or anything else that could be humorous. Deep breathing – from your diaphragm – helps people relax. *See page 65* .

The Roman poet **Horace** (65-8 BCE) said

"When angry, count to ten before you speak; if very angry, one hundred!"

Try counting to ten before saying anything. This may not address the anger directly, but it can minimize the damage you will do while angry.

Objectives

Make things easier on yourself, leave the area, take a brisk walk, and return when you are calm. You will find it much easier to deal with the situation in an appropriate manner. Examine the issue and deal with it. Learn to act and not re-act.

No matter how stupid or inconsiderate you perceive the situation to be, ask yourself **"Have I ever done that?"**. Try to look at the situation from the other viewpoint, it maybe they just made an error of judgement – something you can rest assured that you have been guilty of at some point.

Ask yourself this question: **"Will the object of my anger matter ten years from now?"** Chances are, you will see things from a calmer perspective. Be honest with yourself. Do not ignore the problem as ultimately it could prove fatal – **literally!**

Take regular physical exercise. Cycling, swimming, and walking can all keep you trim and will aid chemical imbalances.

Engage in self-improvement activities such as reading, courses and seminars. Learn to adopt a positive mental attitude. You will be amazed at the changes you can make in your life by 'changing your thinking'.

Consider using subliminal relaxation audio mp3/CDs. These have been shown to have a beneficial effect on people. The great thing with these products is that they can accessed at any time that is suitable or convenient to you i.e., bedtime, whist jogging or during a lunch break.

Never give up!

If you think you may have difficulty in altering or controlling your behaviour then seek the help of your doctor or qualified therapist. The important thing is to not leave your negative emotions bottled up. There is no shame in protecting your own health or improving your lifestyle. This benefits not only you but those around you.

Anger Management Therapy

Anger Management Therapy is a corrective and helpful approach for controlling and anger. The objective is to confront the causes and deal with it in a safe and appropriate manner, in order that it is not destructive to the individual or the safety of other 's around them. Anger is often a result of feelings blocked or frustrated by something the subject holds to be important, or by a situation that gives rise to feelings of powerlessness. Anger management isn't just a matter of distancing oneself from the object of anger (although that may help in certain circumstances) rather it's about finding the appropriate or alternative channels of expression. Identifying what provokes an emotional outburst, exploring those triggers that turn anger into full blown rage in greater detail.

This allows for a three-dimensional perspective on situations and events whereby, the anger can escalate and allow them to confront and successfully deal with them rather than just reflexively reacting. Anger management aims to develop self-awareness and a complete understanding of their emotions and its effect on others. It is based upon the premise that our bodily and emotional responses are shaped by underlying, evolutionary psychological scripts.

Anger management classes are available in most areas as well as online video courses. These classes teach you how to react differently to various situations including the things you should avoid doing such as: -

* **Don't Try to do everything at once!** Set small targets for tasks that you can easily achieve.

* **Don't focus on things that you cannot change!** Focus your time and energy on your own wellbeing.

* **Don't believe yourself to be alone!** Most people get angry at times and support is always available.

* **Don't use stimulants!** Such as Alcohol, Cigarettes or Drugs to relieve anger – these can all contribute to poor mental health.

Classes differ in length from one week to three months. Some focusing exclusively on recognizing and describing your triggers, whilst others go into greater detail and provide different methods and approaches in dealing with them. In addition, there are also classes that teach specific skills in assertive communication and assertive behavioural management.

You may require individual therapy to learn new techniques and ways of using your skills so that you gain a more positive perspective on life. Whilst one to one (individual) therapy can be expensive, there are several free anger management programs that you can try at home. In certain cases, anger management classes may require a combination of individual and group therapy. These groups can help you learn new social and communication skills, as well as new ways of relaxing and building self-confidence.

Should you decide to try anger management therapy, you should be aware that it has its own set of benefits and disadvantages. One advantage is that you will be able to control your emotions, allowing you to better handle your environment and those around you. When you achieve control over your emotions, you can then progress further by making positive changes in your life. Another advantage is that behavioural changes can be made in relatively short period of time in just a matter of weeks or months.

Many people who go for this therapy, find that they immediately experience a reduction in their level of stress, which helps them live a better, more fulfilling life and improve their mental health.

However, there are also drawbacks to this type of behavioural change. The disadvantages are that it can take a long time to identify your own specific anger triggers, and make the required changes into your life, such as developing new and better life habits, eliminating the undesirable and unwanted ones. In addition, you may also have to consider your domestic and workplace environments. Difficulties at home i.e., caring for another adult or, at work where you may have been subjected to bullying will all be factors that will contribute to your wellbeing mental health. Nevertheless, you do not have to do this on your own as help will always be available.

(CBT) Cognitive Behavioural Therapy is an effective form of anger management and a popular alternative to psychotherapy. **(CBT)** therapy involves identifying a positive way to channel your negative feelings, instead of letting them build up and eventually turning into a full-blown rage.

See Page 51 for further information.

Breathe in, Breathe out

Many people who suffer from panic attacks tend to over breathe even when they are not experiencing a panic attack.

Learning some good breathing techniques can really help to reduce the lightheaded feeling that **hyperventilation** brings, often accompanied by a tight sensation in the chest when experiencing a panic attack. For most people this is the first and worst stage of the attack, imagining their heart is unable to cope, or they are going to faint or even die. Deep, slow breathing techniques can reduce the sensations of panic in the body. and help to focus on their breathing instead of the thought processes (spiralling out of control). It helps to overcome the waves of panic and regain control. With practice the sufferer can eventually stop the cycle from reaching that unbearable stage.

Getting the breathing under control is a key factor, as it is both a symptom and a cause of the panic attack, so it's important to address to address it.

> *"I discovered a simple solution to my panic attacks was to focus on my breath, breathing in deeply and slowly then pushing my breath out consciously on the exhale. I would repeat a phrase (Which I made up) over and over again, to focus my breathing. I later discovered this phrase was also an ancient Buddhist saying that was developed for meditation. I would think "breathe in love" on the inhale, and "breathe out fear" on the exhale. It would stop the panic attack from taking root and I learnt to use it the first hint of an attack, each time I started to move into that cycle."*

– Emma Chilster (34)

It is important to first realize that hyperventilating is giving the lungs too much **Oxygen** and reducing the blood levels of **Carbon Dioxide (CO2)** The lungs are absorbing the Oxygen <u>too fast</u>, and do not have enough Carbon Dioxide to counteract it. This results in the body being unable to maintain the correct chemical balance, leaving the person feeling short of air.

If during a panic attack you feel lightheaded, dizzy, short of breath and numb in your extremities with a tight chest and a thumping heart, then you are hyperventilating. In addition, you may also experience clammy hands, a dry mouth and feel as if you are breaking into a sweat. You could be shivering and feel weak all over. You may want to sit down.

Breathing evenly and regularly will dissipate the problem. Below are a couple of easy methods to help you do this.

Belly Breathing

Babies Belly-Breathe naturally. If you observe a sleeping baby, you will notice that it is their tummy that rises and falls with each breath – NOT their chest.

Normal Belly Breathing

Take a deep breath in through <u>**your nose**</u> filling your tummy area completely allowing the air to travel all the way to your diaphragm. Your belly should expand by 3-6cm. Your chest should remain flat and still. Exhale out fully through <u>**your nose.**</u> As you breathe out pull your belly in towards your spine. Take in another deep breath and continue to breathe deeply. Each time you exhale, aim to exhale <u>fully</u> for twice as long as you inhale. This deep breathing allows the oxygen in your body to access the areas and places where it is most needed. Each inhale and exhale count as one cycle. Try to repeat the cycle 5 times then once you have done it a few times then try to repeat the cycle 10 to 20 times.

Deep Breathing to Calm Down Anxiety

Known as the **4-7-8** Method.

As shown above, Inhale slowly, this time counting to **4** through **your nose** and hold onto it for **7** seconds. Then where this method differs from the *'Belly Breathing Method'* above, slowly let the air **out of your mouth** counting to **8**, again pulling your tummy in towards your spine to help you expel as much air as you can.

Repeat the cycle four times or more if required.

This method is also particularly useful in helping you to sleep.

Yoga – Your Way Out

Yoga, Tai Chi and Pilates not only help you shape and define your body, but make you focus on relaxing and your general body awareness. Meditation and massage also help relax the muscles and reduce the tension we can so easily build up before a panic attack. Add some sort of relaxation into your day every day. Make it part of your everyday process. At the very least your body will thank you for it.

Yoga your way out...

Will I Need Medication?

If your panic attacks are happening frequently enough to impede your everyday life or you are experiencing four or more attacks a month, then it is important that you seek professional help.

The most important aspects of this are: -

* It will give you confirmation and clarity of any condition diagnosed and

* Peace of mind – Thus alleviating further anxiety.

Whilst many self-help techniques can help you to avoid the experience of panic attacks, it is of the utmost importance that you receive as much help as you can get. Like many conditions, the earlier it is diagnosed the easier it is to treat without the possible long-term effects disrupting your life.

Regardless of the advice you receive, or medication prescribed, it is important to remember that you are still the one in charge. Weigh up the pros and cons of each treatment and consider if it is something that will work for you. Many people find a multi-faceted approach to solving their panic attacks works best using a range of solutions to keep it all in check.

Anti-depressants

Many doctors will prescribe sufferers of regular panic attacks antidepressants. These help around fifty to sixty percent of patients. While these were developed for depression, being prescribed them doesn't mean your doctor thinks you are depressed, anti-depressants have also been found to work with people suffering from anxiety/panic attacks.

Anti-depressants work by working with your **Serotonin** levels in the brain which have been found to relate to your feelings of panic. It is not a quick fix solution, with the antidepressants taking two to four weeks to take effect. Many people will stop taking them after a few days as they feel their symptoms may become worse and they aren't working. It is important that the patient perseveres and allows time for the drug to take effect.

Serotonin (Also referred to as the 'Happiness Hormone') is made via a unique biochemical conversion process. It begins with **Tryptophan**, an essential amino acid that is present in differing amounts, in all protein foods. This amino acid is the building block for the neurotransmitter **Serotonin**. The cells that make **Serotonin** use **Tryptophan Hydroxylase**, a chemical reactor and when combined with **Tryptophan**, forms **5Hydoxytryptamine**, (otherwise known as **Serotonin**) a type of chemical that helps relay signals from one area of the brain to another. Although **Serotonin** is manufactured in the brain, where it performs its primary functions, some 90% of our **Serotonin** supply is found in the digestive tract and in blood platelets. Changes in the levels of **Serotonin** can alter the mood and is often credited with the feelings of wellbeing.

There are a range of different anti-depressants available and it can take time to discover which one suits your metabolism and needs best. All of them do have side effects and it is up to you to consider whether these are worth experiencing as you take the drug.

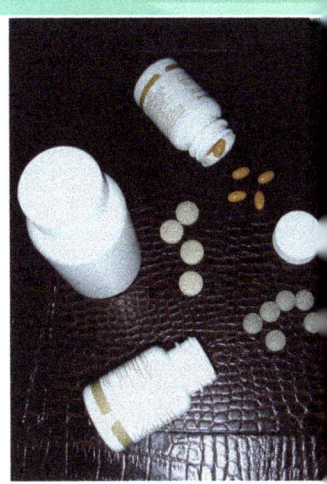

Happiness is...

when what you think, what you say, and what you do are in harmony

- Mahatma Gandhi -

Selective Serotonin Reuptake Inhibitor (SSRI)

SSRIs are a type of anti-depressant drug that inhibits the reabsorption of serotonins by neurons, increasing the availability of Serotonin as a neurotransmitter. **SSRIs** should **NEVER be taken or prescribed without a full and thorough prognosis carried out by a qualified medical practitioner.**

SSRIs are the most common type of drug prescribed for anxiety/panic attacks, as these have been devised explicitly to affect **Serotonin** levels. **SSRIs** are known to be beneficial and research statistics show they can help up to 70% of patients. However, **SSRIs** are **NOT SUITABLE FOR EVERYONE** and cannot be used for some specific pre-existing medical conditions such as **Bi-polar Disorder, Epilepsy, Haemophilia, Types 1 & 2 Diabetes** or taken alongside some medications.

In addition, certain types of **SSRIs** have known unpleasant side-effects when too much Caffeine (found in coffee and Energy drinks) is consumed, such as Nausea, Restlessness, Insomnia or Palpitations.

It is important to allow **2-3 weeks** for them to take effect and you should liaise closely with your Doctor during this period. Sudden withdrawal of the drug can have adverse effects.[5] Recent research has suggested that the taking of **SSRIs** may cause birth defects. Ensure that you notify your Doctor if you believe you are pregnant so that any risk can be professionally assessed.

If you have been diagnosed with an **Anxiety/ Panic Disorder**, it is expected you will need to take an anti-depressant for at least a year. Weaning yourself off them is a slow process and needs to be done under the close supervision of a doctor to ensure that you do not damage the progress you have made by withdrawing from them too fast. Around half of the people who wean themselves off them, revert to having panic attacks again. For these people, taking the drug long term is the preferred option.

If you have had **CBT (Cognitive Behaviour Therapy)** during your time on anti-depressants you are less likely to return to having anxiety/panic attacks once you stop the medication.

Taking Control and Moving Forward

Foods That May Enhance Your Anxiety

It is not my intention to weigh the reader down with huge amounts of information (most of which is available from the local library, your dietician / nutritionist, or the worldwide web). However, an understanding of how these products can and do affect people will hopefully help them to avoid the pitfalls.

If you have a particular sensitivity to a certain type of food, consuming it can increase the likelihood of having an anxiety/panic attack. There are a few types of foods that can trigger an attack but specifically there are three main types that can affect your ability to control your anxiety and keep any resultant attack in check.

The top three anxiety producing foods are sugar, alcohol, and caffeine. These do not directly cause a panic attack, but they can increase your general state of anxiety which can compound the problem.

Sugar

How interesting it is that one of the groups of foods that <u>we do not need</u> to supplement our diet is sugar? Unlike proteins and fats added sugar is not essential for good health. For millennia humans evolved with the only sugars being available for nutrition were those extracted from fruit, vegetables (tubers) and nectar (Honey), which in many cases would have only been available seasonally!

Eating relatively small amounts of sugar along with the accompanying fibre would have offset any possible adverse effects of the **Fructose** found within fruit and to a lesser degree vegetables. Whilst Honey which contains several types of sugars (mostly made up with **Fructose** and **Glucose** along with traces of vitamins and minerals), tastes much sweeter than Table Sugar (**Sucrose** – a combination of Fructose and Glucose).

Sugar is an addictive substance and apart from the obvious problems of tooth decay and excessive weight gain (**Obesity**), sugar can cause chemical imbalances within the body, anxiety, difficulties with concentration, hyperactivity (Sugar Rush) and aggravate or worsen the symptoms of **ADHD (Attention Deficit Disorder)** in children.

How sugar is used in the human body and its effects!

Human beings can do very well without added sugar. There is no Recommended Daily Allowance (**RDA**) for sugar. Many experts believe that we can do without it completely. Monitor how many calories you are consuming and what quantity of those are carbohydrates, fats, and proteins. There are natural sugars in vegetables and fruit. People today consume large of amounts of sugar, and not just in the obvious things like sweets and chocolates. There are significant amounts of sugar used in processed foods and some foods from 'Fast Food' restaurants. As children, we became used to the taste and then demanded the same (or more) as adults. This behaviour in turn is passed to our children and so the cycle continues. There are some manufacturers and producers who are now beginning to actively remove or lessen the amount of sugar used in their products. The problem is that they stand the risk of lower sales (because of the change in taste) and in some cases use sugar substitutes which may be even more hazardous to health.

The intake of sugary food needs insulin to counteract it in the bloodstream. The body releases large amounts of insulin that reduces the amount of sugar in your blood. Unlike **Glucose**, **Fructose** (The sugar found in fruit, vegetables and extensively used in processed foods) can only be processed through your liver. When your system becomes overloaded, specific enzymes in your liver are activated that then convert the **Fructose** into fat. This then raises the **Triglyceride** levels in the bloodstream which subsequently can lead to weight gain (**Obesity**) and insulin resistance.

Interestingly, most people believe that Sugar can create a wave of mood changes including a state of hyperactivity (referred to as a 'Sugar Rush') The actual evidence of this is almost non-existent, despite many controlled experiments both in Europe and the USA. Whilst sugar intake will increase the bodies levels of insulin, no correlation has shown that the ingestion of sugar alone can lead to a 'sugar rush'. However, a sensible diet is everything, the craving for sugar foods or high carbs such as doughnuts and cakes may indicate a sugar addiction problem which should be examined. Consuming a lot of sugar can also cause lactic acid to build up in your bloodstream. High levels of this can bring on chemical changes within your body and actively produce a state of anxiety resulting in a panic attack. If you tend to suffer from panic attacks, it is a good idea to go on a low **Glucose** or low sugar diet. As refined carbohydrates also convert to sugar fast, it is best to stick to natural foods with plenty of whole grain, vegetables, and good protein.

Alcohol

Alcohol is a stimulant and exaggerates the senses. It fools you into believing your senses are enhanced when in reality your performance, cognitive and physiological reactions are seriously undermined. Brain cells, unlike others, do not regenerate and consistent drinking can and does result in irreparable damage. Alcohol (like excessive sugar intake) can also increase the levels of lactic acid in your body. It also prevents you from being able to make reasoned decisions or informed judgements clearly. The long-term effects of alcohol consumption such as ***Cirrhosis*** of the liver, mouth cancers etc... are well known. Perhaps a fact that is not widely recognised is that the cost of treating Alcohol related sickness is climbing alarmingly – recently estimated at £3 billion a year in the UK.

Caffeine

Caffeine may make you feel like you are getting started in the morning, but it can be wreaking havoc with your ability to handle stress and your levels of anxiety. Caffeine can block the protein **Adenosine** which regulates the ring of neurons in the brain. This protein is the one that causes you to feel drowsy. Caffeine directly affects its ability to kick start the process, increasing the ring of the neurons. This makes your body produce adrenaline because your body thinks an emergency is close by. The adrenaline increase can cause your heart rate to increase and elevate your body's state of emergency. This can be enough to make you feel anxious.

Caffeine also increases the lactic acid build up in your body. If you think you are drinking too much caffeine from both coffee and carbonated caffeine drinks such as energy drinks and cola, then **slowly** reduce the amount you are drinking to remove the problem.

Moderation is Key

Watch your caffeine intake from all sorts of sources – i.e., Green Tea, which has good health benefits, contains substantial amounts of **Theanine** which increases **Alpha** brain waves and inhibits tension/anxiety making **Beta** waves. However, it also has a high amount of caffeine. Like all things in life, moderation is the key.

Reduce the use of Stimulants. We've talked about the impact of alcohol, caffeine and sugar on people who suffer anxiety/panic attacks.

Avoiding these things will check the chemical imbalances within the brain. It is also a good idea to check whether medications you are prescribed contain stimulants. Even cold and flu medication can often contain large amounts of stimulants that will trigger anxiety/panic attack, as will some diet pills.

Stress Busting Foods that lead to a healthier lifestyle.

The timing of meals can be quite critical to good health and well-being. Match your mealtimes with your daily activity. As a rule, remember it is better to eat small portions on a regular basis (Little and Often) than large meals once or twice a day. Also put simply, if you are going to do little physical exercise then eat likewise (A little), only consume enough fuel for the energy you will use. So, don't 'blow out' an hour or so before bedtime and don't 'make do' with a candy bar or packet of crisps if you are going to engage in sports or other physical exertions (Such as heavy manual work) during the day.

A major nutritional mistake is that many people skip breakfast, whether they are just too busy or have got out of the habit or worse still, quite wrongly believe that skipping breakfast will help weight management issues. Skipping breakfast denies the body of the supply of essential nutrition in providing the energy required for the day. If continued, this can result in long term serious health issues as the body will extract the resources it needs from the body, depleting essential nutrients and vitamins (such as Vitamin B complex), creating difficulties in maintaining the correct levels of blood sugar. This will inevitably lead to greater degrees of chemical imbalance within the body and contribute to feelings of frustration and stress.

This is particularly important to women suffering with stress (particularly those with poor or inadequate diets and reliance upon high daily intakes of caffeine and/or cigarettes) inhibiting the absorption of minerals such as calcium which is absolutely essential to the body.

Lack of calcium will result in the body depleting its own reserves leading to a net loss of bone mass. This condition is called **Osteopenia** which can lead to **Osteoporosis**, or porous bone. [6] This condition is responsible for thousands of bone fractures in women (aged on average 40+) every year.[7] Low levels of blood calcium can also result in **Hypertension** (High Blood Pressure) and Colon Cancer.

Avoidance of these conditions is relatively straightforward. Consumption of calcium rich foods, such as hard fruits, sesame seeds, milk, beans, dried small shrimps, kelp, and celery. The addition of Vitamin D (produced by UV rays (sunlight) acting on the skin also contributes to the production of calcium. Vitamin D also is available as an addition to products such as Soya milk, some fish such as Tuna, Salmon and Mackerel. These fish are also rich in **Omega 3** and **Tryptophan.**

Supplements can also be used such as Deva Calcium-Magnesium Plus and Vega Calcium plus Vitamin D. The body's ability to absorb calcium does lessen with age. However, you should always consult with your Doctor before taking supplements and of course some conditions such as those that suffer with High Cholesterol or certain allergies will limit what foods should or can be consumed.

Mixed Nuts and Seeds such as Almonds, Walnuts, Brazil Nuts and Pumpkin Seeds contain vitamin E and other minerals like Magnesium and Zinc whilst fruits such as Oranges, Papaya, and berries are loaded with vitamin C.

Dark Cocoa Chocolate Content 70% plus will give you the benefits of eating chocolate without the resultant 'low' experienced with normal chocolate. The higher the Cocoa content the better. Dark chocolate is known to increase the **serotonin** levels in the brain and in addition can boost the amounts of **serotonin** in the gut which can strengthen the immune system.

Small amounts of chocolate or chili peppers can also be attributed with enhanced secretion of endorphins giving the feeling of comfort and well-being. However, moderation is key as otherwise your intake of caffeine will also increase dramatically.

Decaffeinated Black Tea (unsweetened) lowers the levels of the stress hormone **Cortisol.** All teas from the **Camellia** tea plant are rich in polyphenols, which are a type of antioxidant. The caffeine content in this tea is 0-12mg per 240ml as opposed to the normal 14-16mg.[8] If you suffer from headaches, restlessness, or anxiety you should consider cutting back your intake more than 500mg per day.

Water – drinking about 500g before going for a brisk walk aids blood movement and stimulates the brains 'Happy' chemicals, the non-addictive endorphins (Neurotransmitters) which help to de-stress you. These were only identified as recently as 1975 and may be nature's own cure for high levels of anxiety and stress.

Food for Thought

This piece was sent to me as part of an anonymous article and I became intrigued. I have found references to the piece on the net, but I was unable to find the author's name. I kept it for future reference. Whilst the author appears to have matched certain appearances to particular foods i.e., contrived content, the overall message of eating healthier is sound. It is certainly true that there are other foods that will supply the same nutrients. Still, it is still Food for Thought!

> "It's been said that the Creator first separated the salt water from the fresh, made dry land, planted a garden, made animals and fish...and all before making a human being. He made and provided what we'd needed before we were created. These are best & more powerful when eaten raw. We're such slow learners...So the Creator left us a great clue as to what foods help what part of our body!
>
> A sliced Carrot looks like the human eye. The pupil, iris and radiating lines look just like the human eye... And YES, science now shows carrots greatly enhance blood flow to aid function of the eyes.
>
> A Tomato has four chambers and is red. The heart has four chambers and is red. Research shows tomatoes are loaded with the antioxidant **lycopene** and are indeed pure heart and blood food. Grapes hang in a cluster that has the shape of the heart. Each grape looks like a blood cell and scientific studies show that grapes are also profound heart and blood vitalizing food.

A Walnut looks like a little brain, a left and right hemisphere, upper cerebrums, and lower cerebellums. Even the wrinkles or folds on the nut are just like the neo-cortex. We now know walnuts help develop more than three dozen neuron-transmitters for brain function. Kidney Beans heal and help maintain kidney function and yes, they look exactly like the human kidneys.

Celery, Bok Choy, Rhubarb and many more look just like bones. These foods specifically target bone strength. Bones are 23% Calcium, and these foods are 23% Calcium. If you don't have enough Calcium in your diet, the body pulls it from the bones, thus making them weak. These foods replenish the skeletal needs of the body.

Avocadoes, Eggplant and Pears target the health and function of the womb and cervix of the female – they look just like these organs. Today's research shows that when a woman eats one avocado a week, it balances hormones, sheds unwanted birth weight, and helps prevents cervical cancers. And how profound is this? It takes exactly nine (9) months to grow an avocado from blossom to ripened fruit. There are over 14,000 photolytic chemical constituents of nutrition in each one of these foods (modern science has only studied and named about 141 of them).

Figs are full of seeds and hang in twos when they grow. Figs increase the mobility of male sperm and increase the numbers of Sperm as well to overcome male sterility.

Sweet Potatoes look like the pancreas and balance the glycaemic index of diabetics.

Olives assist the health and function of the ovaries.

Oranges, Grapefruits, and other Citrus fruits look just like the mammary glands of the female and assist the health of the breasts and the movement of lymph in and out of the breasts.

Onions look like the body's cells. Today's research shows onions help clear waste materials from all the body cells. They even produce tears which wash the epithelial layers of the eyes. A working companion, Garlic, also helps eliminate waste materials and dangerous free radicals from the body."

As stated, I think there is some artistic licence here but overall, there is nothing that I can see that will do any harm – not withstanding allergies and pre-existing medical conditions.

Which would YOU rather be?

Positive and Optimistic

Negative and Pessimistic

Taking Control and Moving Forward

Stress is a normal part of daily life. It's how we react to it that makes all the difference in maintaining our health and well-being.

Pressures occur throughout life and those pressures cause stress. You need to realise that you will never completely get rid of stress in your life, but you can learn coping techniques to turn that stress into a healthier situation.

Positive Mental Attitude

The No.1 criteria for Self-Development and controlling the way that we think, and consequently how we feel. Stress is largely a result of how we perceive a situation or event. Thoughts, whether positive or negative, have a profound influence on our emotions and our resulting behaviour.

Is your glass half full or half empty?

Negative thoughts generally result in a pessimistic attitude. Creating tensions both physically and emotionally. This increases the difficulties in controlling our abilities to exert controls over a given stressful situation or event. Increasing levels of stress can cause health problems including panic attacks or anxiety disorders. This repetitive train of thought can lead to further negative emotions and behaviour, whereby medical depression may be subsequently diagnosed.

You may have heard the saying *"What comes around goes around"* or *"What you put out you will receive"* more often known as the **'Law of Attraction'**. These deal with the fact that both negative and positive thoughts and actions affect both the individual and those around them.

Positive thoughts, however, promote feelings of optimism, well-being, and general good emotional and physical health. Social and emotional benefits become more evident i.e., improved harmony in personal and professional relationships and a happier more satisfying lifestyle. Levels of stress appear to become much reduced (even disappear) but more importantly, our ability to control our reaction to stress is greatly enhanced. If you are the type of person that finds it difficult to cope with stress or tends to withdraw from their environment and immerses themselves further into their problem(s). The afore mentioned approach alone may not be the optimum direction for you. Resultant loss of work (Money) and friends (Support) will add considerably to existing stress factors.

Serious consideration should be given to creating a personal support network. This can be made up of close friends, relatives and / or guidance counsellors (Where necessary). Talking with your support network can greatly disperse tension, boost problem solving and provide distractions from your own situation. If you don't know how to organise a support group or just need to talk to someone then do contact your local GP's surgery where you would normally find access to people who will be happy to help you. Remember the adage

'A problem shared is a problem halved'.

Smile. Nothing is more universally recognizable than a smile. A smile, even by a stranger can uplift your mood instantly and make you feel happy. The amazing thing is when you smile back in return you are having the same effect on them. The feelings of happiness which are generated by smiling, is not coincidental. Smiling transmits signals via the facial nerves to sections of the **Limbic System** and trigger **Endorphins** (Often referred to as the brain's 'Happy Chemicals') which have a chemical structure similar to Morphine and Codeine and are one of a group of **Neuropeptides** which give us a non-addictive 'high'. Evidence shows that these enhance health and success and can be acted upon.

Apart from the extremely rare condition Moebius Syndrome (whereby sufferers are physically unable to smile). Most people can smile albeit that some people may find it difficult. If you are one of those that find it difficult to smile, there are several techniques that you can use to help:

* Smile at the mirror and your own reflection – How do you imagine you appear?

* What direction is your hair and what colour is it? Do you have any freckles, moles, or beauty spots? If so, precisely where? What colour are your eyes?

* Now, what do you look like when you smile? Every time you see a reflection of yourself in the mirror or reflective glass – **SMILE!**

* Imprint upon your memory the last image that you saw, was **YOU SMILING!**

Repeat this as often as you can, even if it is a quick glimpse out of the corner of your eye. The more you see yourself smiling the more you will smile and feel happy and positive about yourself.

Smile With Confidence!

Try this simple technique to boost your confidence, hold a pencil or pen between your teeth (Across from cheek to cheek). Try it now!

As you can see and feel, this simple action forces your mouth and face to smile, and bizarre as it sounds, holding this position for just 60 seconds, has been shown to have a real effect on your emotional happiness levels – those Happy Chemicals again!

Conversely, try doing the same exercise but with the pen or pencil between your top lip and the base of your nose. As you will now feel, this forces your face into a frown and guess what, in a short while you will experience a real downturn in your mood.

Saying 'cheese' really does have a purpose but do try to smile with your eyes first, otherwise you run the risk of producing a grimace rather than a full rounded smile.

Laughter is the next step up from smiling. At its root it represents our fundamental need for human connection. Shared feelings of camaraderie, trust, security, and a sense of belonging, all contribute to the basic need for the physical and emotional experience of human connection. Recalling memories of happy events can produce the physiological experiences that were experienced at the time of the original event.

Laughter (even more than smiling) is contagious. As an example, try the following exercise: -

Known as 'Laughter RX' – Stand in front of a mirror and 'belly laugh' three times each day for at least 15 seconds at a time. It is very important to approach the task with gusto and not a little snicker or timid chuckle. Wherever possible, do this in the company of others. You will find that initially friends and family may laugh <u>at you</u> but pretty soon they will be laughing <u>with you</u>. The laughter producing Endorphins are shown to be physically and emotionally beneficial. Proof (if proof were needed) that

'Laughter is undoubtedly the best medicine'.

Music and Relaxation

Note the two titles go hand in hand. Obviously, the type of music being listened to, the environment in which it is being listened to, and the individuals' personal preferences will all have an effect.

Baroque music such as that by Mozart and Handel, have been shown to have amazing effects on relaxation, sleep learning and increased sense of intuition and concentration. This is achieved by the music's ability to organize neuron ring patterns in our cerebral cortex and assist both the left- and right-hand side of our brains, helping us to overcome the typical left-brain dominance in our modern society.

Listening to **Baroque** music slows our heartbeat, our blood pressure decreases, beta (fast) brain waves slow down by about six percent while alpha brain waves (the slow kind) increase as much. This allows the synchronization of both brain hemispheres. The resulting effect is also called **alert relaxation**. In this state of conscience our body is more efficient and able to function on less output of energy. This is one reason that calming background music is used in Surgical Theatres, it not only benefits the patient but the theatre staff as well.

Conversely, Music such as Heavy Rock, Techno or Rap are more likely to produce an excited or aggressive state, leading to increased levels of **Adrenalin** and therefore impact or aggravate existing stressors further. General physical health can also be affected i.e., studies have shown that the consumption of food will be quicker, and the amount eaten considerably increased.

Listening Environment

Relaxing music therapy can truly help a person to unwind. The environment needs to be conducive to relaxation and act as a conduit to dissipate your stress levels.

Find a space where you can be fully at ease. Plan to be totally immersed in the task with no interruptions either by outside disturbances or personal needs i.e., refreshments or mobile phone etc…

You could also consider using aroma candles and subtle lighting, but don't overdo it, you don't want to swamp the senses. The core objective is to lie down and become totally relaxed, letting yourself submit to the natural ebb and ow of the waves of calming music.

Close your eyes, take a deep breath (from your diaphragm right up into your chest), slowly inhale through your nose then hold (For the count of 5) then slowly exhale through your mouth.

Repeat this three times.

Whilst doing this try to visualize a relaxing scene such as lying on the beach or a grassy meadow. Focus on the details i.e., the sounds and smells. You will be pleasantly surprised at where your mind can lead you. To reach the full effect of relaxation normally takes around 30 minutes of listening (dependant on the individual).

There are many different types of relaxation music commercially available, such as those that include the sounds of Waterfalls, Oceans, Whale song, Nature and Chanting. Alternatively, you may wish to consider Auto Suggestion / Hypnosis music albums that are now widely available. As well as specific programs for stress relief these can also be used for all aspects of self-improvement.

If you plan to do this on a regular basis it will be worth building up your own collection ensuring that the time taken to produce the desired result is maximized to your benefit.

Leave Your Job At Work

Don't take your job (and its associated worries and concerns) home with you. Office politics have no place in your home or with your family. Take the decision to create specific clear-cut boundaries between work and home – don't take anything to do with work into your home, no laptop, phone, or files. If these are shared with your personal items, then create separate folders and access numbers. Make the process of accessing work information at home, time consuming and laborious – you will soon get fed up trying to 'quickly' look at your inbox or load spreadsheets.

If you are one of those people who routinely take work home with them and/or has a never ending 'To Do' list, then you may need to look at your **Time Management** Skills. There are numerous articles, courses, and seminars available that cover Time Management. It really is worth investing some of the time that you spend on the 'To Do' list on investigating the options available to you. Adverse feelings of being pressurised and overworked often lead to anxiety attacks and ultimately lead to loss in confidence and performance.

Exercise and Take Care Of Yourself

According to recent statistics the percentage of people in the UK now overweight (Obese) has increased to over 50% of the population in the last 10 years! Exercise can massively reduce the impacts of chronic health conditions and help the related stress caused. Physical exercise reduces the stress related tensions in your body and helps to correct chemical imbalances. It also promotes the natural 'feel good' chemicals (Endorphins) in your body. You don't have to 'Go Mad' and blindly over-exert yourself. Always remember to do warm up exercises first, then slowly build up a program of exercises that will take up about 20 minutes of your time. There are exercise regimes for everybody regardless of age or sex. However, you should consult your Doctor if you have any medical conditions that may limit or preclude your ability to participate in physical exercise – **Before Attempting it!**

We can all help ourselves by doing the simple things like walking instead of taking the car, not spending as much time sitting and watching the television or on the computer. Taking turns walking the dog (If you have one). Watching what and when you eat. Make sure you don't skip breakfast. Eat an apple instead of a packet of crisps. Try a bowl of vegetable noodles instead of Double Burger and chips. Choose high fibre Brown bread (made of the entire wheat grain which is high in vitamins) or Crispbread instead of highly processed (Bleached) White bread. Cut down on tea and coffee, and drink plenty of water. You can't pick up a magazine, look at the internet or TV without seeing tips on how to do more exercise and lose weight. We cannot say we were not told and therefore have no-one to hold responsible for our health but ourselves.

Involve yourself with a hobby or pastime, apart from the obvious distractions from stressful situations or events that may continue to confront us. A hobby or pastime can completely remove us from the perceived stress. It often requires us to concentrate on other things, other people, or other problems. Forcing us to put to one side our own difficulties or issues. Whether, it is a game of golf, gardening, or alternatively something creative such as painting or sculpture. The point is that it is all absorbing. The emotion, pace and result of our effort will emanate from within us. The passion, ambition, and satisfaction of achievement (no matter how small) will fill us with a sense of pride and wellbeing, actively demonstrating our own ability to conquer our fears and control our responses; based on the knowledge attained and the confidence we have gained in ourselves.

Make Exercise fun – A Fantastic Way to Get Rid of Stress

Go for a run, on your own or with a friend. Running makes your heart rate go up and you'll be using up all that adrenaline too.

Regular exercise also helps you to reduce stress levels overall.

'Walking for Health'

This group are enjoying a walk through the local countryside near the village of Weston, Northants, England. There are lots of walking/hiking groups throughout the world who arrange walks just like this that offer not only health benefits but also social benefits too.

Cycling

Cycling is considered a 'low impact' exercise, with the saddle and handlebars providing some support, and is a great way to exercise and meet new friends. You should start off gently and increase slowly. There are cycling clubs all over the world.

The **CTC** – Cycling Touring Charity – founded in 1878 with around 70,000 members holds tours and events all over the U.K.

Swimming

Swimming is also classed as 'low impact' sport. This is because the water supports the body, and it is a very good exercise for your limbs and lungs as well as keeping you trim.

Local leisure centres often have several classes for all levels – from novices to the more experienced. Another advantage of swimming is that it is a sport that can benefit the whole family, no matter what age or ability and creates a perfect opportunity for the family to spend more time together and to encourage each other.

To keep the body in good health...
is a duty, otherwise we shall not be able to keep our mind strong and clear.

– Buddha –

Smoking

Smoking is detrimental to our well-being, and certainly does affect our health adversely. Smoking is known to trigger the symptoms of anxiety and panic attacks as it narrows the blood flow and increases the levels of adrenaline. Recent research has shown that a 30-year-old male smoker is more likely to **die** on average **18 years earlier** than a 30-year-old non-smoker. Unnecessary deaths from lung cancer, other cancers, heart disease, strokes, chronic bronchitis, and other respiratory diseases can all be **avoided by NOT smoking**. Like all unwanted habits, giving up is not easy, it is an addictive habit. There is now a lot of help and guidance available (often free of charge!) as well as numerous products and services available commercially.

Try the following if you are serious about quitting:

- **Put together a plan** of action.

- **Identify those times** when you smoke or develop cravings – plan for 5-minute substitutions i.e., Washing Up, Taking the dog for a walk, going for a run, Indoor Exercising, Gardening, Washing the car or a hobby that requires both hands.

- **Examine your diet** and routine – Certain foods and daily routines are mentally associated with smoking.

- **Decide to stop** smoking indoors or in the car.

- **Consider and prepare** snack substitutions for cigarettes – i.e., cheese biscuits, mints, fruit, or gum.

- **Set a specific** date that apart from the normal day to day stresses does not present any additional difficulties.

- **Discard all evidence** or material traces of cigarettes and ashtrays etc…

- **Go for it!**

**** Good Luck! ****

Xscape Anxiety

Conclusion

Anxiety attacks are experienced by a huge range of people from all walks of life. However, they don't need to be a life sentence, they can be controlled. The knowledge of the symptoms and causes can assist us in improving our general health and lifestyle.

Thank you for taking the time to read my book, for which I am most grateful. I would like to wish you every success in your own journey towards a greater understanding of the subject. I hope that my efforts here will help alleviate your fears of the unknown and enable you to become all that you can or wish to be.

Jonathan Powell

*"Take care... of your body,
It's the only place you have to live"*

– Jim Rohn –

Acknowledgments

Thank you to all my friends, family and acquaintances who helped me with their views, opinions, and ideas to produce this book.

My special thanks to: -

Sally Aquire whose articles helped me and many others, to understand and appreciate in simple terms those who experience **OCD**.
Andrew Reynolds, Will Edwards, Ayd Instone and Richard McCann who inspired me to take positive action and assist me in my life's journey. To the following experts who through their articles in the public domain allowed me and others to benefit from their contributions.

(1) **Douglas Mennin PHD** – Psychologist ADADA

(2) **Kate Tilmouth** RCN, CPD

(3) **Mark Bresnan** – Psychologist Bath University

(4) **Dr James L Wilson** – DC, ND, PHD – Integrative.psychiatry net

(5) **Dr Tim Kendall** -Dir.Nat.Coll.Centre (Mental Health); Author and collaborator for **N.I.C.E.** Guidelines.

(6) **The National Osteoporosis Society**

(7) **Prof. E. Kampman** – Article for University of Maryland Medical Centre.

(8) **Mayo Clinic**

(9) **T C Photography** – For the photographic contributions

www.toricfotographi.blogspot.com

(10) **Mrs Victoria Cordell** – for creative and editorial assistance.

And finally, to my wife **Doreen**, who has always supported me without question, regardless of understanding or interest in my various projects.

For New Updates and Advice
http://www.arete-publishing.com/blog

The People Who Help People to Help Themselves!

www.ingramcontent.com/pod-product-compliance
Lightning Source LLC
LaVergne TN
LVHW010317070426
835507LV00026B/3431